Master Math at Home

Data and Measurement

Scan the QR code to help your child's learning at home.

mastermathathome.com

How to use this book

Math — No Problem! created **Master Math at Home** to help children develop fluency in the subject and a rich understanding of core concepts.

Key features of the Master Math at Home books include:

- Carefully designed lessons that provide structure, but also allow flexibility in how they're used.

- Speech bubbles containing content designed to spark diverse conversations, with many discussion points that don't have obvious "right" or "wrong" answers.

- Rich illustrations that will guide children to a discussion of shapes and units of measurement, allowing them to make connections to the wider world around them.

- Exercises that allow a flexible approach and can be adapted to suit any child's cognitive or functional ability.

- Clearly laid-out pages that encourage children to practice a range of higher-order skills.

- A community of friendly and relatable characters who introduce each lesson and come along as your child progresses through the series.

You can see more guidance on how to use these books at **mastermathathome.com**.

We're excited to share all the ways you can learn math!

Math — No Problem!
mastermathathome.com
www.mathnoproblem.com
hello@mathnoproblem.com

First American Edition, 2022
Published in the United States by DK Publishing
1745 Broadway, 20th Floor, New York, NY 10019

22 23 24 25 26 10 9 8 7 6 5 4 3 2 1
002–327149–Nov/2022

This book was made with Forest Stewardship Council™ certified paper—one small step in DK's commitment to a sustainable future. For more information go to www.dk.com/our-green-pledge

Published in Great Britain by Dorling Kindersley Limited

A catalog record for this book is available from the Library of Congress.

ISBN: 978-0-7440-5203-9
Printed and bound in China

For the curious
www.dk.com

Acknowledgments

The publisher would like to thank the authors and consultants Andy Psarianos, Judy Hornigold, Adam Gifford, Dr. Wong Khoon Yoong, and Dr. Anne Hermanson.

The Castledown typeface has been used with permission from the Colophon Foundry.

Contents

Ruby   Elliott   Amira   Charles   Lulu   Sam   Oak   Holly   Ravi   Emma   Jacob   Hannah

Understanding Tables

Starter

Miss A'liya and Miss Fathima look at the gym timetable to plan which classes to go to.

Class	Start Times		Duration (min)	Location
	AM	PM		
Superspin	9:35, 11:15	1:05, 5:50	35	Room 2 (Level 3)
Skiparama	6:05, 8:25, 10:10	8:45	30	Room 3 (Level 1)
Stretchathon	7:35, 11:15	4:55, 9:25	45	Room 5 (Level 2)
Up and Down		1:50, 7:10, 10:05	40	Room 1 (Level 3)
Twist 'n' Turn	8:10, 9:10	1:15	60	Room 4 (Level 1)

*Please arrive at the exercise class 5 minutes before the start time.
**Allow 2 minutes to travel between each floor.

If Miss A'liya and Miss Fathima want to go to 2 classes each, which classes could they choose?

Example

Miss A'liya wants to go to Superspin and Skiparama in the morning.

If I go to the 9:35 a.m. Superspin class, can I go to the 10:10 a.m. Skiparama class?

Miss A'liya needs to allow 4 minutes to travel between 2 floors.

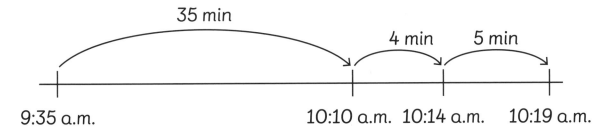

35 min   4 min   5 min

9:35 a.m.   10:10 a.m.   10:14 a.m.   10:19 a.m.

Miss A'liya needs to be at the 10:10 a.m. Skiparama class 5 minutes before it starts at 10:05 a.m. She cannot attend both the 9:35 a.m. Superspin and 10:10 a.m. Skiparama class.

Miss Fathima plans to go to the 11:15 a.m. Stretchathon class and stay at the gym for lunch. She will then go to the 1:50 p.m. Up and Down class.
How much time will Miss Fathima spend at the gym?

Find the duration of time from when Miss Fathima arrives for the first class to the start of the second class.

She needs to arrive 5 minutes before the first class starts.

5 min   45 min   1 h   50 min

11:10 a.m.   11:15 a.m.   12:00 p.m.   1:00 p.m.   1:50 p.m.

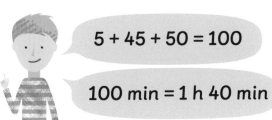

5 + 45 + 50 = 100

100 min = 1 h 40 min

1 h 40 min + 1 h = 2 h 40 min

The duration of time from when Miss Fathima arrives for the first class to the start of the second class is 2 hours 40 minutes.

Add the duration of the Up and Down class.

2 h 40 min + 40 min = 2 h 80 min
= 3 h 20 min

80 min = 1 h 20 min

Miss Fathima will be at the gym for 3 hours 20 minutes.

Practice

Use the table in the Starter section to answer the following questions.

1 Sam's mom starts an Up and Down class at 7:10 p.m.
How long does she have to sit down and rest before she has to leave for the 8:45 p.m. Skiparama class?

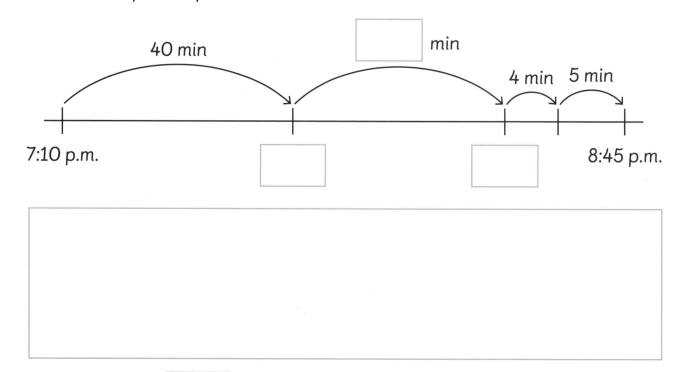

Sam's mom has ☐ minutes to sit down and rest.

2 Mr. Nightingale leaves the gym after he attends the 11:15 a.m. Stretchathon class. If he goes to a Superspin class before he goes to the Stretchathon class, how long is he at the gym?

Mr. Nightingale is at the gym for [ ] hours [ ] minutes.

3 Amira's dad arrives 15 minutes before his Up and Down class starts. He talks to his friend for 55 minutes after the class finishes and then leaves the gym.
How much time has Amira's dad spent at the gym?

Amira's dad has spent [ ] hours [ ] minutes at the gym.

Reading Line Graphs

Starter

Charles recorded the temperature in the school playground at different times in one day.

Time	AM				PM			
	08:00	9:00	10:00	11:00	12:00	1:00	2:00	3:00
°F	52	54	56	58	60	61	61	59

How can we show this information on a graph?

Example

This is called a line graph.

A line graph shows how things change over time.

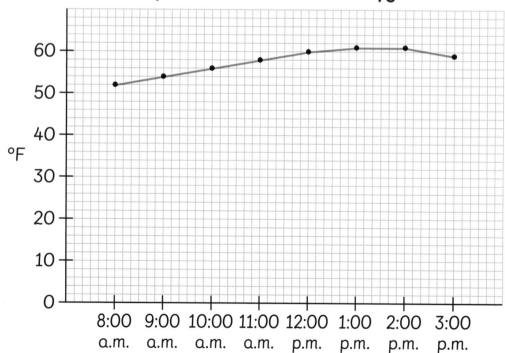

Temperature in the School Playground

I can see when the temperature was at its highest and how quickly it changed.

We can use a line graph to show the information.

The line graph shows the average monthly rainfall in Seattle, Washington.

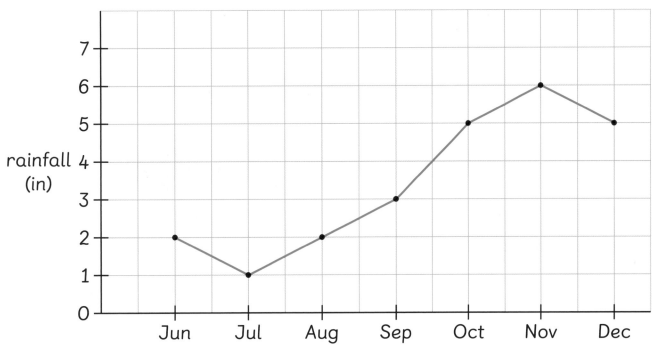

Rainfall in Seattle Over 7 Months

1. Which month had the highest amount of rainfall?

2. Which month had the least amount of rainfall?

3. How many months had an average rainfall of 2 in?

4. By how much did the average rainfall increase between July and September? ___ in

5. By how much did the average rainfall decrease between November and December? ___ in

6. ___ and ___ both had 5 in of rainfall during the 7-month period.

Drawing Line Graphs

Starter

Oak is doing a project for her class on the rising prices for swimming. She made this table to show the changing prices at a public pool over 6 years.

Year	Ticket Price
2017	$3.00
2018	$3.60
2019	$4.20
2020	$5.00
2021	$6.40
2022	$8.00

What types of graphs can Oak use to show this information?

Example

I think Oak should use a bar graph. Bar graphs are good for comparing things.

I think she should try both ways.

A line graph might be better. She wants to show how quickly the price has changed.

I can see the price for each year on the bar graph. It's easy to compare one bar to another.

Public Pool Ticket Price, 2017–2022

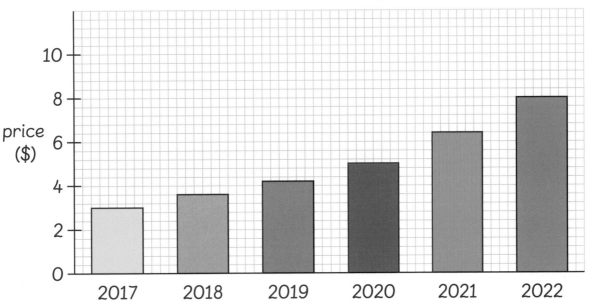

Public Pool Ticket Price, 2017–2022

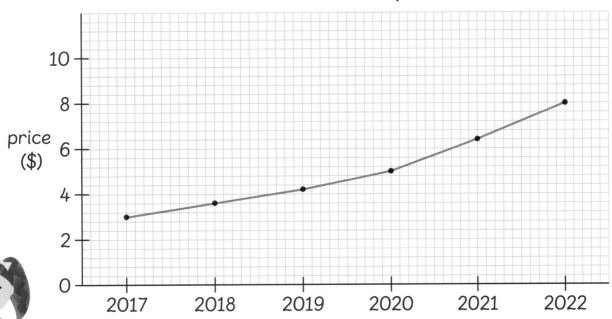

The line graph shows me how quickly the price changed.

When we use a line graph to show how something changes over time we can also call it a **time graph**.

1 The table shows the different prices for a cabin rental over
a period of 8 months.
Draw a line graph using the information in the table.

Month	Apr	May	Jun	Jul	Aug	Sep	Oct	Nov
Price	$65	$75	$90	$110	$135	$95	$90	$75

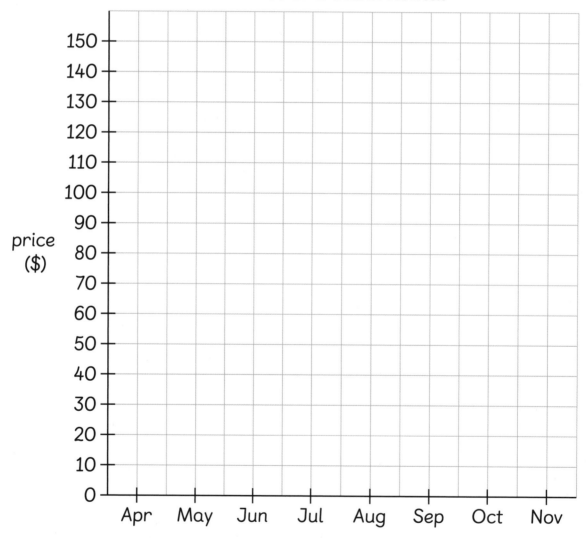

Price of a Cabin Rental

(a) [   ] is the most expensive month.

(b) The largest monthly increase in price is between the month of
[   ] and the month of [   ].

(c) There is a difference of $ [   ] between the most expensive and the least expensive month.

(d) The largest monthly difference in price is between the month of [   ] and the month of [   ] .

2 The table shows the average exchange rate from US dollars to British pounds in a given year. When the exchange rate from US dollars to British pounds is 0.75, it means that $1 would buy £0.75.

Year	2018	2019	2020	2021
Exchange rate	0.75	0.78	0.75	0.72

Draw a line graph using the information in the table.

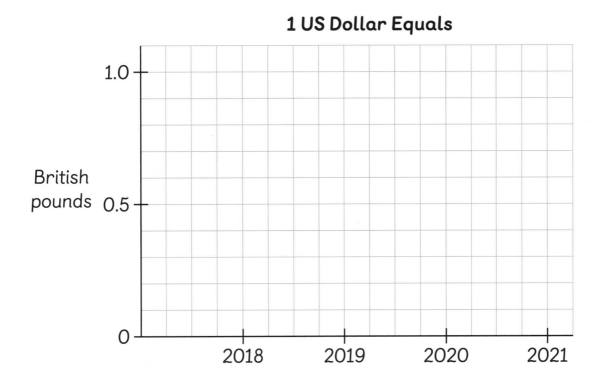

1 US Dollar Equals

Measuring Time in Seconds

Starter

The children timed how long it took to tie their shoelaces.
How long did it take each of them?

Example

We can use a stopwatch to measure time in seconds.

It took Elliott 12 seconds
to tie his shoelaces.

We can use the timer on a cell phone.

It took Ruby 15 seconds
to tie her shoelaces.

14

We can also use the second hand on a clock.

It took Charles 16 seconds to tie his shoelaces.

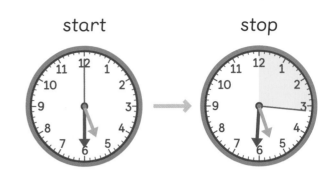
start   stop

Practice

1 Use a stopwatch or the timer on a cell phone to time how long it takes to:

(a) sing Happy Birthday ▢ seconds

(b) hop on one leg 10 times ▢ seconds

(c) recite the alphabet ▢ seconds

2 How many seconds have passed?

(a) start   stop

▢

(b) start   stop

▢

(c) start   stop

▢

(d) start   stop

▢

Converting Time

I took 125 seconds to solve the problem.

I took 2 minutes and 10 seconds to solve the problem.

Who took less time to solve the problem?

We can compare the times using minutes and seconds or using just seconds.

Example

Compare the times using minutes and seconds.

60 seconds = 1 minute
120 seconds = 2 minutes
125 seconds = 2 minutes 5 seconds

We write
2 minutes 5 seconds
as 2 min 5 s.

Sam took 2 minutes 5 seconds.
Lulu took 2 minutes 10 seconds.

Compare the times using seconds.

2 minutes = 120 seconds
2 minutes 10 seconds = 130 seconds

1 minute = 60 seconds

Sam took 125 seconds.
Lulu took 130 seconds.

Sam took less time than Lulu to solve the problem.

1 Convert the following to seconds.

(a) 3 minutes $\boxed{}$ seconds

(b) 2 minutes 25 seconds $\boxed{}$ seconds

(c) 4 minutes 44 seconds $\boxed{}$ seconds

2 Convert the following to minutes and seconds.

(a) 120 seconds $\boxed{}$ minutes $\boxed{}$ seconds

(b) 140 seconds $\boxed{}$ minutes $\boxed{}$ seconds

(c) 190 seconds $\boxed{}$ minutes $\boxed{}$ seconds

3 Holly took 165 seconds to make a smoothie.
Sam took 2 minutes 35 seconds to make a smoothie.
Who took longer to make a smoothie?

$\boxed{}$

It took $\boxed{}$ longer to make a smoothie.

4 Charles wanted to complete a level on his game in under 5 minutes.
He completed the level in 290 seconds.
Did he complete the level in under 5 minutes?

$\boxed{}$

$\boxed{}$

Changing Time in Minutes to Seconds

Starter

Holly skips for 5 and a half minutes. How many seconds are there in 5 and a half minutes?

Example

We need to multiply 60 by 5 to know how many seconds are in 5 minutes.

$60 \times 5 = 300$

One minute has 60 seconds. A half minute is 30 seconds.

We then need to add 300 and 30.
$300 + 30 = 330$

I can use a number line to help me.

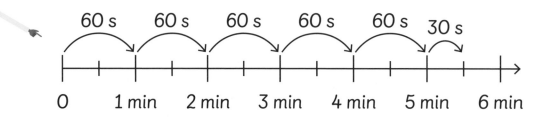

There are 330 seconds in 5 and a half minutes.

1 Fill in the blanks.

(a) 2 min = ▢ s

(b) ▢ min = 240 s

(c) 5 min = ▢ s

(d) ▢ min = 180 s

2 Ravi read his novel for 12 minutes and 40 seconds.
For how many seconds did he read in total?

Ravi read for ▢ seconds in total.

3 Draw lines to match.

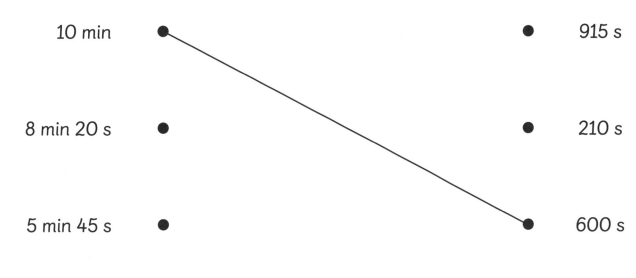

10 min •   • 915 s

8 min 20 s •   • 210 s

5 min 45 s •   • 600 s

$3\frac{1}{2}$ min •   • 500 s

15 min 15 s •   • 345 s

Changing Time in Hours to Minutes

Starter

Ruby was at a theme park for 4 hours and 45 minutes.
For how many minutes was she at the theme park?

Example

1 hour has 60 minutes.
We need to multiply 60 by 4 to work out how many minutes are in 4 hours.
$60 \times 4 = 240$

Next, we need to add 45 minutes to 240 minutes.
$240 + 45 = 285$

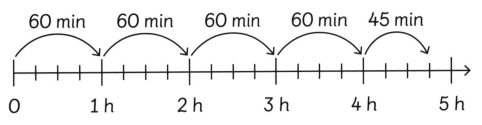

Ruby was at the theme park for 285 minutes.

1 Fill in the blanks.

(a) 3 h = [   ] min   (b) [   ] h = 300 min

(c) 7 h = [   ] min   (d) [   ] h = 660 min

2 The school day is 6 hours and 30 minutes.
How many minutes are there in 6 hours and 30 minutes?

6 h 30 min = [   ] min

3 Draw lines to match.

9 h ●   ● 732 min

8 h 45 min ●   ● 270 min

$4\frac{1}{2}$ h ●   ● 540 min

7 h 10 min ●   ● 525 min

12 h 12 min ●   ● 430 min

Solving Problems on Duration of Time

Lulu's mom roasts a chicken for 90 minutes.
At what time will the chicken be ready if she begins roasting it at 11:45 a.m.?

Example

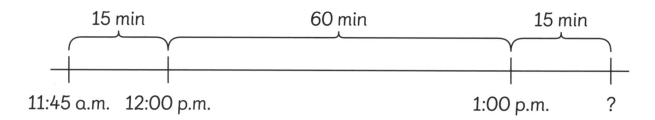

15 min	60 min	15 min
11:45 a.m. 12:00 p.m.		1:00 p.m. ?

The chicken will be ready at 1:15 p.m.

1 Elliott puts a cake in the oven to bake at 10:45 a.m.
He takes the cake out of the oven after 45 minutes.
At what time does Elliott take the cake out of the oven?

[ ] min   [ ] min

10:45 a.m.   11:00 a.m.   [ ]

[ ]

Elliott takes the cake out of the oven at [ ] .

2 Holly got on a train at 4:45 p.m. She got off the train at 6:00 p.m.
How long was her train journey?

New Cross Station

[ ]

Holly's train journey was [ ] hour and [ ] minutes long.

3 Ravi and his family need to arrive at the theater at 6:30 p.m.
The journey from home takes 1 hour and 25 minutes.
At what time should they leave home?

[ ]

Ravi and his family should leave home at [ ] .

Measuring Mass

Starter

A pizzaiolo needs 5.6 kg of flour in order to make pizza dough for the following day.

I have 2 bags of flour with a mass of 2.27 kg and 3 bags with a mass of 454 g.

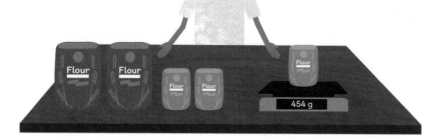

Does she have enough flour to make the pizza dough for the following day?

Example

If we convert all the mass to grams we can add the bags of flour together.

2.27 kg is equal to 2270 g.

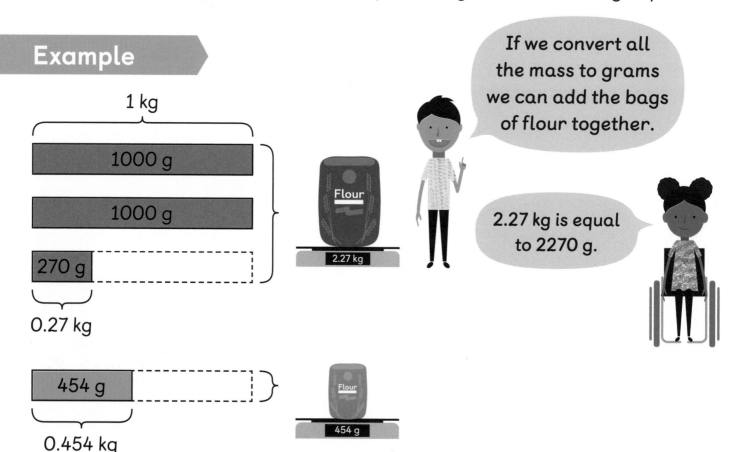

1 kg

1000 g

1000 g

270 g

0.27 kg

454 g

0.454 kg

2.27 kg

454 g

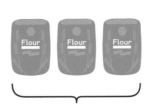

Let's add the mass of the large bags.

We can multiply to find the mass of the smaller bags.

2270 + 2270 = 4540   454 × 3 = 1362

4540 + 1362 = 5902

We can add to find the total mass of all the bags of flour.

5.6 kg is equal to 5600 g.

The pizzaiolo needs 5600 g of flour. She has 5902 g of flour.

She has enough flour to make the pizza dough for the following day.

Practice

Read the scales to find the mass of each item.
Put the items in order from lightest to heaviest.

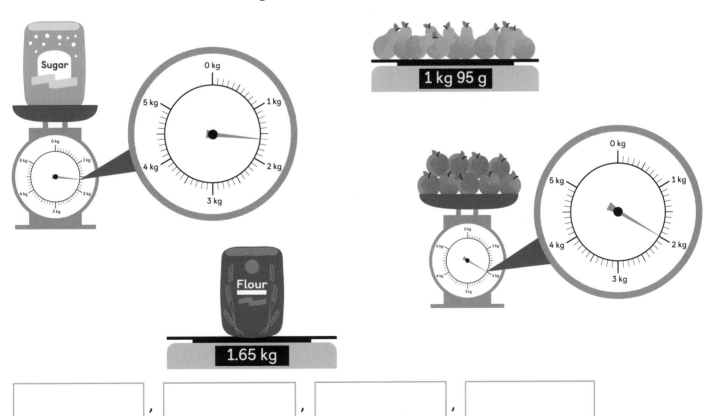

_____ , _____ , _____ , _____

Converting Units of Mass

Starter

Jacob needs to post 2 packages together.
To post them together, the mass of the
2 packages cannot be more than 3.5 kg.
Can Jacob post the 2 packages together?

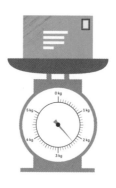

Example

We need to add the mass of the 2 packages.

We can convert
2.3 kg to grams.
2.3 kg is equal
to 2300 g.

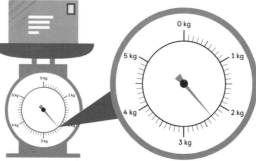

$$
\begin{array}{r}
{}^{1}2\ 3\ 0\ 0 \\
+\quad 8\ 5\ 0 \\
\hline
3\ 1\ 5\ 0
\end{array}
$$

Now we can add. 2300 + 850 = 3150

1000 g = 1 kg, 100 g = 0.1 kg,
10 g = 0.01 kg, 1 g = 0.001 kg

1 kg

| 100 g | 100 g | 100 g | 100 g | 100 g | 100 g | 100 g | 100 g | 100 g | |

10 × 10 g

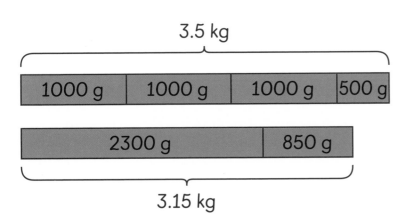

3.5 kg

| 1000 g | 1000 g | 1000 g | 500 g |

| 2300 g | 850 g |

3.15 kg

3150 g is equal to 3.15 kg.

3.15 kg is less than 3.5 kg.
Jacob can post the 2 packages together.

Practice

1 Fill in the blanks.

(a) 2 kg = ⬚ g

(b) ⬚ kg = 2250 g

(c) 3.5 kg = ⬚ g

(d) ⬚ kg = 4050 g

(e) 6 kg 60 g = ⬚ g

(f) ⬚ kg = 10 000 g

2 Circle the lighter package.

2 kg 750 g

2075 g

3 Put these masses in order from heaviest to lightest.

3 kg 300 g   3.03 kg   3033 g

⬚ , ⬚ , ⬚

Measuring Volume

Starter

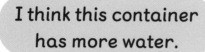

I think this container has more water.

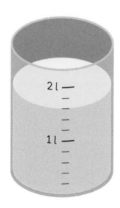

I think this container has more water.

Who is correct?

Example

These containers have markings that tell us how much liquid is inside.

There are 5 steps between each liter on this container. Each mark is 0.2 l.

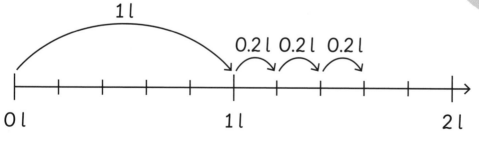

1 l

0.2 l 0.2 l 0.2 l

0 l   1 l   2 l

This container has 1.6 l of water in it.

There are 4 steps between each liter on this container. Each mark is 0.25 l.

Each step is $\frac{1}{4}$. $\frac{1}{4}$ is equal to 0.25.

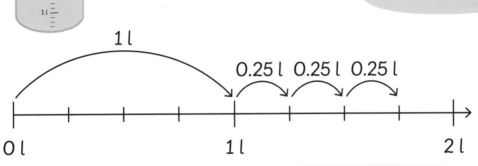

1 l

0.25 l 0.25 l 0.25 l

0 l   1 l   2 l

The shorter container has 1.75 l of water in it. 1.75 l > 1.6 l

Ravi is correct.
The shorter container has the most water.

Practice

What is the volume of liquid in each measuring beaker?

1
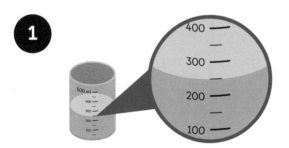

Volume of liquid = ☐ l

2
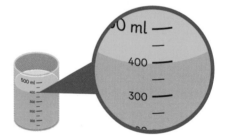

Volume of liquid = ☐ l

3
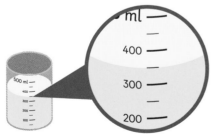

Volume of liquid = ☐ l

4
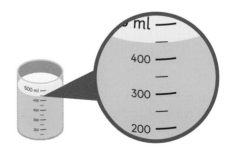

Volume of liquid = ☐ l

Converting Units of Volume

Starter

Which bottle has the greatest volume of liquid?

Example

$1 \, l = 1000 \, ml$

$1.2 \, l = 1 \, l + 0.2 \, l$
$= 1000 \, ml + 200 \, ml$
$= 1200 \, ml$

We can convert the volumes in liters to milliliters.

1 l

1

1000 ml

0.2 l

0.1	0.1

200 ml

30

1 l 136 ml = 1000 ml + 136 ml
$\qquad$ = 1136 ml

950 ml

1200 ml is greater than both 1136 ml and 950 ml.
The bottle of orange juice has the greatest volume of liquid.

Practice

1 Fill in the blanks.

(a) 2 l = [　　　　] ml

(b) [　　　　] l = 1500 ml

(c) 2.25 l = [　　　　] ml

(d) [　　　　] l = 300 ml

(e) 4 l 400 ml = [　　　　] ml

(f) 7.07 l = [　　　　] ml

2 Put these volumes in order from least to greatest.

5.05 l　　　　5500 ml　　　　5 l and 5 ml

[　　　　] , [　　　　] , [　　　　]

Converting Kilometers to Meters

Starter

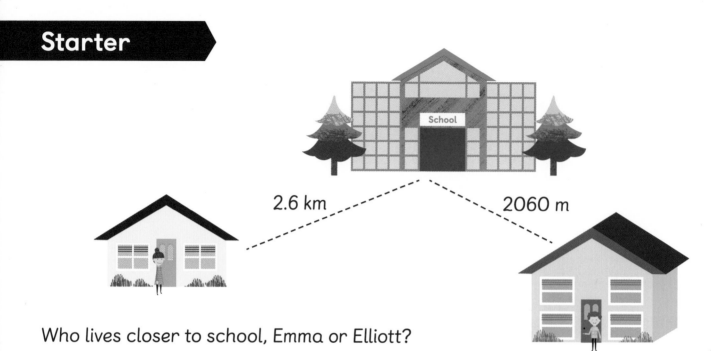

Who lives closer to school, Emma or Elliott?

Example

Convert 2.6 km to meters.

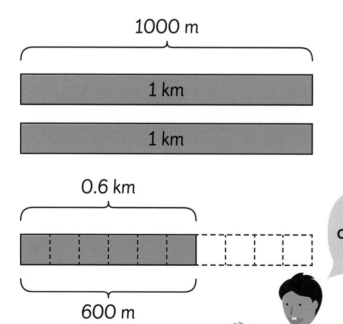

1000 m

| 1 km |
| 1 km |

0.6 km

600 m

Emma lives 2.6 km from school. 2 km is equal to 2000 m.

0.6 km is 6 tenths of 1000 m. It is equal to 600 meters.

2.6 km is equal to 2600 m.

2600 m

2.6 km

2.06 km

2060 m

Emma lives 2600 m away from school.

Elliott lives 2060 m away from school.

Elliott lives closer to school than Emma does.

Practice

1 Fill in the blanks.

(a) 5.2 km = ☐ m

(b) ☐ km = 1250 m

(c) 3 km 750 m = ☐ m

(d) 10.5 km = ☐ m

(e) 10.05 km = ☐ m

(f) ☐ km = 10 005 m

2 On Monday, Jacob walked 3.5 km. On Tuesday, he walked 2900 m. On Wednesday, he walked 600 m further than he walked on Tuesday. How far did Jacob walk over the three days in km?

Jacob walked ☐ km over the three days.

3 Put these distances in order from shortest to longest.

3950 m   3.9 km   3.899 km

☐ , ☐ , ☐

Measuring Length in Feet and Inches

Starter

Mrs. Diaz is decorating for a birthday party. She has a yellow tablecloth that is 48 inches long. She needs the tablecloth to cover a table that is 5 feet long. Will her tablecloth cover the entire table?

Example

Mrs. Diaz can measure the length of the table in feet using a 12-inch ruler.

The ruler has small numbers on it, marked with lines. Each number represents an inch. There are 12 inches in 1 foot.

So, each ruler is one foot long. The table measures 5 feet or 5 rulers long.

In order to compare the lengths of the table and the tablecloth, Mrs. Diaz needs to compare the lengths in the same unit.

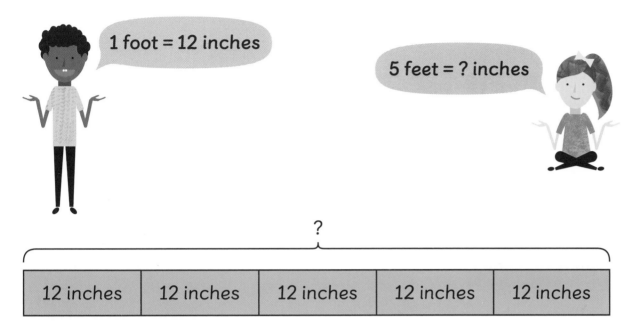

1 foot = 12 inches

5 feet = ? inches

?
12 inches	12 inches	12 inches	12 inches	12 inches

5 × 12 inches = 60 inches

The tablecloth is only 48 inches long, but the table is 60 inches long. Mrs. Diaz's tablecloth is not long enough to cover the table.

Practice

1   Choose the best unit to measure the length of each item.
    Write **inches** or **feet**.

(a)

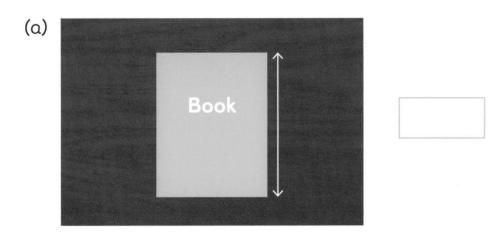

Book

(b)

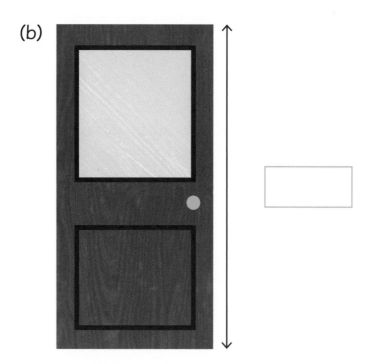

(c)

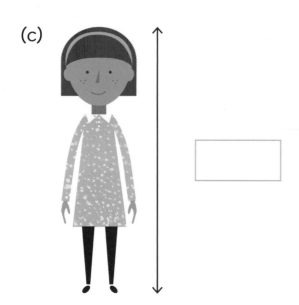

(d)

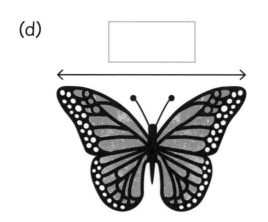

2 Write each length in inches. Use a bar model to help you if needed.

(a) 4 feet = [ ] inches

(b) 3 feet = [ ] inches

3 Compare the lengths using > or <.

(a) 32 inches [ ] 3 feet

(b) 5 feet [ ] 25 inches

(c) 72 inches [ ] 4 feet

(d) 6 feet [ ] 84 inches

4 Amira has a length of ribbon that is 5 feet long.
She needs to use the ribbon to create bows for 4 presents.
For each present, Amira will use 20 inches of ribbon.
Does she have enough ribbon to make bows for all
four presents?

| 20 inches | 20 inches | 20 inches | 20 inches |

Amira [ ] have enough ribbon.

Measuring Weight in Ounces and Pounds

Starter

Ravi is packing his bag for baseball practice. His bag can only hold 4 pounds of gear. The weight of 2 baseballs and his glove are shown below.
Will he be able to carry both the baseballs and his glove in his bag?

Example

First, find the weight of the baseballs.

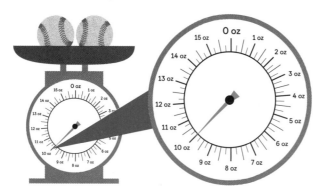

The needle on the scale is pointing to 10 oz.

Oz is short for **ounces**.

The baseballs are being weighed in ounces.

The 2 baseballs weigh 10 ounces.

Each unit is one pound or 1 lb. lb is short for **pounds.**

1 lb + 1 lb = 2 lb

The baseball glove weighs 2 pounds.

To find the total weight of the baseballs and the baseball glove, we can measure them in ounces.

1 lb = 16 oz

2 lb = 2 × 16 oz

    = 32 oz

What is 2 pounds in ounces?

The baseball glove weighs 2 pounds or 32 ounces.

Ravi's bag can hold 4 pounds of gear.

4 lb = 4 × 16 oz

    = 64 oz

The baseballs weigh 10 ounces, and the baseball glove weighs 32 ounces.
32 oz + 10 oz = 42 oz

The baseballs and the baseball glove weigh less than 64 ounces.

Ravi can carry both the baseballs and the baseball glove in his bag.

1 Choose the best unit to measure the weight of each item.
Write **pounds** or **ounces**.

(a)

(b) Flour

(c)

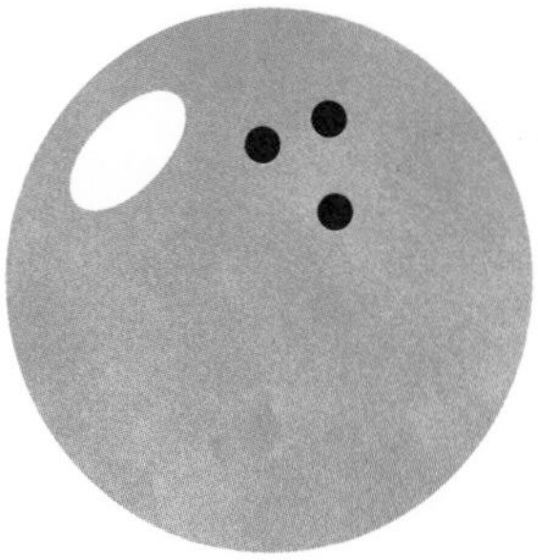

(d)

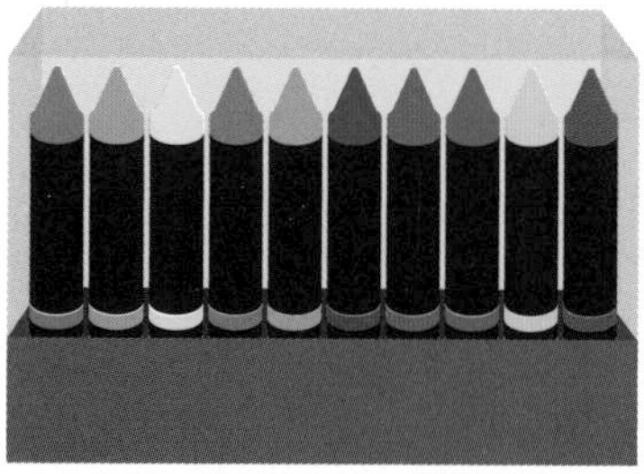

2 Read the scale to find the weight of each item.
Write the weight using **lb** or **oz**.

(a)

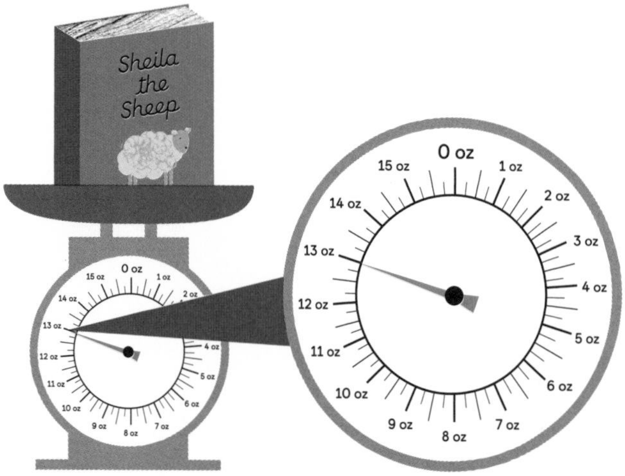

Sheila the Sheep

(b)

[ ]

---

3 Compare the weights using > or <.

(a) 3 pounds [   ] 24 ounces

(b) 32 ounces [   ] 4 pounds

(c) 18 ounces [   ] 1 pound

(d) 5 pounds [   ] 82 ounces

---

4 Jacob says that his baseball bat weighs more than his football helmet.
He says his football helmet only weighs 5 pounds.
His baseball bat weighs 36 ounces.

Is Jacob correct?
Which item is heavier?

[   ]

Jacob [   ] correct.

The [   ] is heavier.

Review and Challenge

1 (a) Draw a line graph to show the information in the table.

Day	°F
1	59
2	59
3	63
4	66
5	52
6	50
7	55
8	63
9	61
10	54

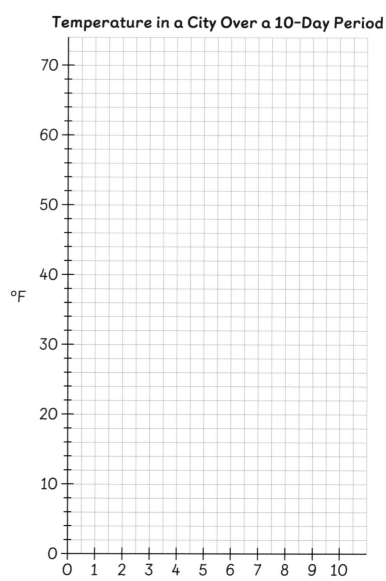

Temperature in a City Over a 10-Day Period

(b) The highest temperature was on day ☐ and the lowest

temperature was on day ☐ .

(c) On how many days was the temperature below 59 °F? ☐

(d) What was the greatest decrease in temperature over two consecutive

days? ☐ °F

2 Jacob started reading at 2:40 p.m. He spent 2 h 35 min reading, then spent some time tidying his bookshelves until 6 p.m.

(a) At what time did he finish reading?

He finished reading at [ ] .

(b) How long did he spend tidying his bookshelves?

He spent [ ] tidying his bookshelves.

3 Sam is posting 3 packages. The mass of the first package is shown. The second package is 500 g heavier than the first package. The third package is 0.25 kg lighter than the first package.
What is the total mass of the 3 packages in kg?

The total mass of the 3 packages is [ ] kg.

4 (a) Ruby spent 35 minutes reading, then she spent $\frac{3}{4}$ of an hour playing soccer. If she started reading at 4:00 p.m., at what time did she finish playing soccer?

Ruby finished playing soccer at ☐ .

(b) Ruby went to sleep at 9:15 p.m. and woke up at 7:30 a.m. For how long did she sleep?

Ruby slept for ☐ hours and ☐ minutes.

5 A train to Chicago from Milwaukee usually leaves the station at 1:30 p.m. The journey should take 125 minutes, but there is a delay of 35 minutes. At what time does the train arrive in Chicago?

The train arrives in Chicago at ☐ .

6 Lulu has 2.5 l of orange juice in a pitcher.

(a) How many 300-ml glasses can she fill with the orange juice?

Lulu can fill ☐ 300-ml glasses with the orange juice.

(b) How much orange juice will be left over?

There will be [ ] ml of orange juice left over.

7 Find the volume of water in each measuring beaker.

(a)

Volume of water = [ ] l

(b)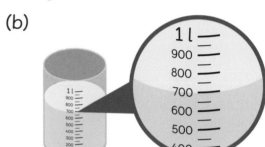

Volume of water = [ ] l

(c)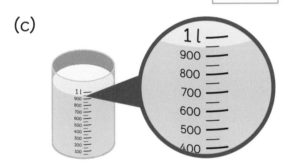

Volume of water = [ ] l

(d)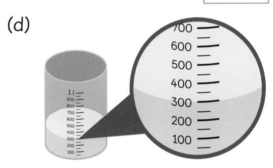

Volume of water = [ ] l

8 Choose the best unit to measure the length of each item.
Write **inches** or **feet**.

(a) length of a bed [ ] .

(b) length of pencil case [ ] .

(c) height of desk [ ] .

Answers

Page 6   **1**

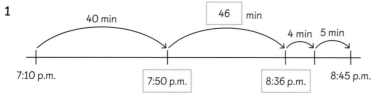

Sam's mom has 46 minutes to sit down and rest.

Page 7   **2**

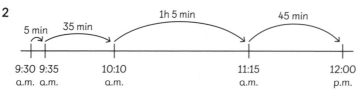

1 hour 5 minutes = 65 minutes
5 + 35 + 65 + 45 = 150
150 minutes = 2 hours 30 minutes.
Mr. Nightingale is at the gym for
2 hours 30 minutes.

3 15 + 40 + 55 = 110; 110 minutes = 1 hour 50 minutes. Amira's dad has spent 1 hour 50 minutes at the gym.

Page 9   **1** November **2** July **3** 2 **4** 2 in **5** 1 in **6** October and December both had 5 in of rainfall during the 7-month period.

Page 12   **1**

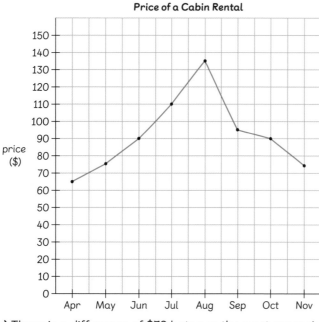

(a) August is the most expensive month.
(b) The largest monthly increase in price is between the month of July and the month of August.

Page 13   **(c)** There is a difference of $70 between the most expensive and the least expensive month.
(d) The largest monthly difference in price is between the month of August and the month of September.

2

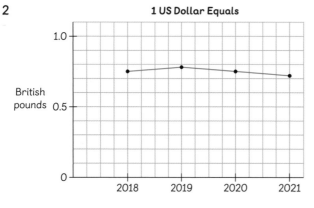

Page 15　**1** Answers will vary.　**2 (a)** 20 seconds　**(b)** 30 seconds　**(c)** 35 seconds　**(d)** 15 seconds

Page 17　**1 (a)** 180 seconds　**(b)** 145 seconds　**(c)** 284 seconds　**2 (a)** 2 minutes 0 seconds　**(b)** 2 minutes 20 seconds
(c) 3 minutes 10 seconds　**3** It took Holly longer to make a smoothie.　**4** 5 minutes = 300 seconds. 290 < 300.
Yes, Charles completed the level in under 5 minutes.

Page 19　**1 (a)** 2 min = 120 s　**(b)** 4 min = 240 s　**(c)** 5 min = 300 s　**(d)** 3 min = 180 s　**2** Ravi read for 760 seconds in total.
3

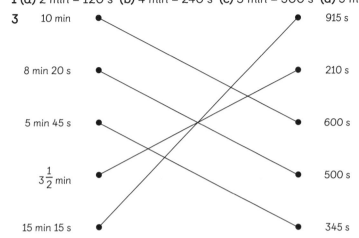

Page 21　**1 (a)** 3 h = 180 min　**(b)** 5 h = 300 min　**(c)** 7 h = 420 min　**(d)** 11 h = 660 min　**2** 6 h 30 min = 390 min
3

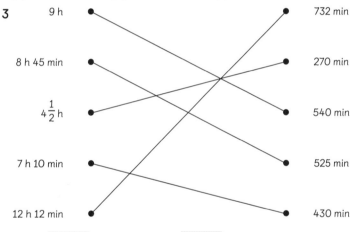

Page 23　**1**

Elliott takes the cake out of the oven at 11:30 a.m.　**2** Holly's train journey was 1 hour and 15 minutes long.
3 Ravi and his family should leave home at 5:05 p.m.

Page 25　sugar, flour, pears, apples

Page 27　**1 (a)** 2 kg = 2000 g　**(b)** 2.25 kg = 2250 g　**(c)** 3.5 kg = 3500 g　**(d)** 4.05 kg = 4050 g　**(e)** 6 kg 60 g = 6060 g

(f) 10 kg = 10 000 g　**2**　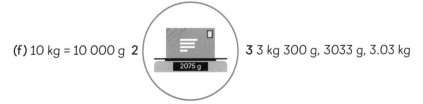　**3** 3 kg 300 g, 3033 g, 3.03 kg

Page 29　**1** 0.25 l　**2** 0.4 l　**3** 0.35 l　**4** 0.45 l

Page 31　**1 (a)** 2 l = 2000 ml　**(b)** 1.5 l = 1500 ml　**(c)** 2.25 l = 2250 ml　**(d)** 0.3 l = 300 ml　**(e)** 4 l 400 ml = 4400 ml
(f) 7.07 l = 7070 ml　**2** 5 l and 5 ml, 5.05 l, 5500 ml

Answers continued

Page 33   **1 (a)** 5.2 km = 5200 m **(b)** 1.25 km = 1250 m **(c)** 3 km 750 m = 3750 m **(d)** 10.5 km = 10 500 m
(e) 10.05 km = 10 050 m **(f)** 10.005 km = 10 005 m **2** Jacob walked 9.9 km over the three days.
3 3.899 km, 3.9 km, 3950 m

Page 35   **1 (a)** inches

Page 36   **(b)** feet **(c)** feet **(d)** inches

Page 37   **2 (a)** 4 feet = 48 inches **(b)** 3 feet = 36 inches **3 (a)** 32 inches < 3 feet **(b)** 5 feet > 25 inches
(c) 72 inches > 4 feet **(d)** 6 feet < 84 inches **4** 5 feet = 60 inches, 4 × 20 inches = 80 inches. 80 inches > 60
inches. Amira does not have enough ribbon.

Page 40   **1 (a)** ounces **(b)** pounds **(c)** pounds **(d)** ounces **2 (a)** 13 oz

Page 41   **(b)** 3 lb **3 (a)** 3 pounds > 24 ounces **(b)** 32 ounces < 4 pounds **(c)** 18 ounces > 1 pound
(d) 5 pounds < 82 ounces **4** 5 pounds = 80 ounces, 80 ounces > 36 ounces. Jacob is not correct.
His football helmet is heavier.

Page 42   **1 (a)**

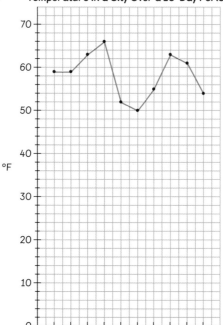

(b) The highest temperature was on day 4 and the lowest
temperature was on day 6. **(c)** 4 **(d)** 14 °F

Page 43   **2**

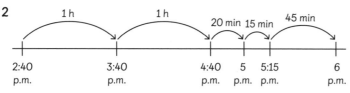

(a) He finished reading at 5:15 p.m.
(b) He spent 45 minutes tidying his
bookshelves.

3 The total mass of the 3 packages is 11.5 kg.

Page 44   **4 (a)** Ruby finished playing soccer at 5:20 p.m. **(b)** Ruby slept for 10 hours and 15 minutes.
5 The train arrives in Chicago at 4:10 p.m. **6 (a)** Lulu can fill 8 300-ml glasses with the orange juice.

Page 45   **(b)** There will be 100 ml of orange juice left over. **7 (a)** 0.55 l **(b)** 0.7 l **(c)** 0.95 l **(d)** 0.3 l
8 (a) feet **(b)** inches **(c)** feet